GW00497267

The Big Book of
Mothers' Wit and Wisdom

First published in 2007 by
PRION
an imprint of the
Carlton Publishing Group
20 Mortimer Street
London W1T 3JW

Some of the material in this book was previously published by Prion in 2006 in *Mothers' Wit*

A catalogue record for this book is available from the British Library.

ISBN 978 1 85375 638 2

Typeset by E-Type, Liverpool
Printed in Dubai

The Big Book of Mothers' Wit and Wisdom

Humorous Quotes on Mums and Motherhood

Compiled by Allison Vale and Alison Rattle

Contents

Introduction

The dictionary definition of the word 'mother' is 'A female who has given birth to offspring.' A truism, yet woefully incomplete. To be a mother is a woman's greatest vocation in life, for mothers make the world go around – literally.

The word mother is linked intrinsically to images of babbling babes in arms, wind-fresh laundry, steamy kitchens, the smell of Dettol, the taste of toffee, the feel of a warm, soft bosom and the touch of deft hands which create, nurture and protect.

How many women spent many a tortured hour in adolescent years, longing for the glory of curing cancer, the fame of the movie star, the adulation of the music industry or the giddy heights of academic brilliance? How many set out to achieve the luminosity of stardom in the first unsteady steps into adulthood? By their thirties, how many more have discovered instead the intensity of their child's first steps across the living room and into their arms?

You set out wanting the world to worship the ground you walk on and pretty soon you realize that motherhood brings with it your own little world that will do exactly that … At least until that little world grows into spotty, hairy and misunderstood adolescence: all pop stars and pop tarts and black hair dye. (At this point you may find yourself wondering what was so bad about the curing cancer idea after all … and so nature turns full circle.)

It's tempting to see motherhood as an art – and one that we have only just begun to grasp in recent times. Medieval motherhood was simply a question of mating, gestating and liberating, followed by an extended period of breastfeeding. Wasn't it?

Teachers asked in the 1940s to comment on the most serious disciplinary issues they faced on a regular basis listed litter and untucked shirts as top gripes. Imagine that. Today's teachers, asked the same question, list violent crime, suicide, drug and alcohol abuse as theirs. So what – or who – is to blame?

Today's mother faces an overwhelming barrage of advice. Education, Western wealth and technological advances mean that women are faced with gargantuan choices to make about every issue from conception on. The path she chooses to take on her child's dad, diet, diapers and dance class is analysed and, inevitably, criticized. However carefully she makes these decisions, if she listens long enough, someone, somewhere, will be bitching.

The truth, for those wanting to discover it, is that motherhood has never been easy: toddlers have always been trouble; teenagers have always been foul; mothers-in-law have always been judgemental and dreaded.

This collection of mothers' wit delves into the heart of motherhood, the joys of which include catching a child's vomit in your hands and cleavage in an attempt to save the carpet, to the more serene moments of guiltily lapping up daytime telly while breastfeeding a newborn.

A mother lies at the heart of every person and we track her development from single woman searching for a potential mate to the white-haired matriarch doling out nuggets of wisdom.

We don't attempt to glorify the mother – after all, no mum is perfect and some are far from it. Instead we capture a mother's foibles, from hatred of housework and ineptitude in the kitchen to dealing with discipline and the guilt of going out to work. Of course there are sprinklings of the soppy and sentimental too, as we cannot help but love our mums!

Here, the combined wit and wisdom of great characters in history, from to Picasso to Presley, Churchill to Reagan, the Marquis de Sade to Dame Edna, testify to the emotional minefield that is motherhood. A mother's influence has moulded the most powerful people on earth and even prompted presidents to form lifelong opinions on broccoli.

Motherhood Is ...

... going back to work for the rest.

Anon.

... the best all round job. No other career would allow you to be plumber, drill sergeant, nurse, chef, umpire, banker, telephonist and international diplomat – all before 9.30 a.m.

Anon.

... mind-blowing.

Britney Spears

... perhaps the only unpaid position where failure to show up can result in arrest.

Mary Kay Blakely

... a wonderful thing. What a pity to waste it on the children.

Judith Pugh

... the keystone of the arch of matrimonial happiness.

Thomas Jefferson

The story of a mother's life: Trapped between a scream and a hug.

Cathy Guisewite

The Best of Times, the Worst of Times

Sometimes the strength of motherhood is greater than natural laws.

Barbara Kingsolver

There never was a child so lovely, but his mother was glad to get him asleep.

Ralph Waldo Emerson

Be nice to your children, for they will choose your rest home.

Phyllis Diller

To be effective and gain the respect she needs to function, a mother must have her children believe she has never engaged in sex, never made a bad decision, never caused her own mother a moment's anxiety, and was never a child.

Erma Bombeck

All my life I've felt like somebody's wife, or somebody's mother or somebody's daughter. Even all the time we were together, I never knew who I was. And that's why I had to go away.

Joanna Kramer, Kramer vs Kramer

I think motherhood makes you apathetic because you're always so tired. I don't know how anyone can march or be politically active when they've only had three hours' sleep.

Jo Brand

You cannot even simply become a mother any more. You must choose motherhood.

Eleanor Holmes Norton

I remember opening the refrigerator late one night and finding [I had chilled] a roll of aluminium foil next to a pair of small red tennis shoes … I quickly closed the door and ran upstairs to make sure I had put the babies in their cribs instead of the linen closet.

Mary Kay Blakely

What Makes a Mother?

A woman has two smiles that an angel might envy, the smile that accepts a lover before words are uttered, and the smile that lights on the first-born babe, and assures it of a mother's love.

Thomas C. Haliburton

I will fight for my children on any level so they can reach their potential as human beings and in their public duties.

Princess Diana

The heart of a mother is a deep abyss at the bottom of which you will always find forgiveness.

Honoré de Balzac

A mother is the truest friend we have, when trials heavy and sudden, fall upon us … [she will] endeavour by her kind precepts and counsels to dissipate the clouds of darkness, and cause peace to return to our hearts.

Washington Irving

There's a lot more to being a woman than being a mother, but there's a lot more to being a mother than most people suspect.

Roseanne Barr

A mother's arms are made of tenderness and children sleep soundly in them.

Victor Hugo

Biology is the least of what makes someone a mother.

Oprah Winfrey

A mother who is really a mother is never free.

Honoré de Balzac

Mother: The most beautiful word on the lips of mankind.

Kahlil Gibran

Most mothers are instinctive philosophers.

Harriet Beecher Stowe

A Freudian slip is when you say one thing but mean a mother.

Anon.

Mothers are a biological necessity; fathers are a social invention.

Margaret Mead

Mother is the dead heart of the family, spending father's earnings on consumer goods to enhance the environment in which he eats, sleeps and watches the television.

Germaine Greer

The ideal mother, like the ideal marriage, is a fiction.

Milton R. Sapirstein

We really have no definition of mother in our law books.
Mother was believed to have been so basic that no definition was
deemed necessary.

Marianne O. Battani

She discovered with great delight that one does not love one's
children just because they are one's children but because of the
friendship formed while raising them.

Gabrel Garcia Márquez

A mother is like a teabag – you never know how strong she is
until she gets in hot water.

Anon.

That dear octopus from whose tentacles we never quite escape,
nor in our innermost hearts never quite wish to.

Dodie Smith

The greatest love is a mother's; then comes a dog's, then comes
a sweetheart's.

Polish proverb

If Heaven decides to rain or your mother to remarry, there is no way to stop either.

Chinese proverb

The kind of power mothers have is enormous. Take the skyline of Istanbul – enormous breasts, pathetic little willies, a final revenge on Islam. I was so scared I had to crouch in the bottom of the boat when I saw it.

Angela Carter

When I Became a Mother
I Learned That ...

... punching your sister in the face can happen accidentally.

... stretch marks last for ever.

... hamsters are more resilient than they look.

... the leading brand of washing powder does not remove all stains.

... as soon as you pass the last motorway station for ninety miles, someone will need the loo.

... I don't have to use a road map – I can just use the veins on my legs.

... an Oscar is never more deserved than by a child just asked to clean her room.

... it's no good crying over spilled baby cereal on a wicker chair.

... bags under the eyes do not disappear until three years after your last child leaves home.

... mothers alone hold the secret recipe for refilling icecube trays.

... valuable pieces of artwork don't cost a penny.

All anon.

The Vetting Process

A girl can wait for the right man to come along, but in the meantime that still doesn't mean she can't have a wonderful time with all the wrong ones.

Cher

I married the first man I ever kissed. When I tell this to my children they just about throw up.

Barbara Bush

Personally, I think if a woman hasn't met the right man by the time she's 24, she may be lucky.

Deborah Kerr

The first time you buy a house you see how pretty the paint is and buy it. The second time you look to see if the basement has termites. It's the same with men.

Lupe Velez

I'm trying to find a man to share my life with, but it's not been easy. I'm a 35-year-old woman with two small children.

Nicole Kidman

This 'relationship' business is one big waste of time. It is just Mother Nature urging you to breed, breed, breed. Learn from nature. Learn from our friend the spider. Just mate once and then kill him.

Ruby Wax

Before I met my husband I'd never fallen in love, though I'd stepped in it a few times.

Rita Rudner

I require three things in a man. He must be handsome, ruthless and stupid.

Dorothy Parker

The trouble with some women is they get all excited about nothing – and then they marry him.

Cher

A man on a date wonders if he'll get lucky. The woman already knows.

Monica Piper

Bigamy is having one husband too many. Monogomy is the same.

Erica Jong

Men should be like Kleenex, soft, strong and disposable.

Cher

It's slim pickings out there. When you're first single, you're so optimistic. At the beginning you're like: I want to meet a guy who's really smart, really sweet, really good-looking, has a really great career ... Six months later, you're like: Lord – any mammal with a day job!

Carol Leifer

Feeling Broody?

We in the West do not refrain from childbirth because we are concerned about the population explosion or because we feel we cannot afford children, but because we do not like children.

Germaine Greer

My husband and I are either going to buy a dog or have a child. We can't decide whether to ruin our carpet or ruin our lives.

Rita Rudner

Our bodies are shaped to bear children, and our lives are a working out of the processes of creation. All our ambitions and intelligence are beside that great elemental point.

Saint Augustine

At the age of 16, I was already dreaming of having a baby because I felt myself to be an adult, but my mum forbade it. Right now, I feel like a teenager and I want to have fun for one or two more years before starting a family.

Milla Jovovich

The one point on which all women are in furious secret rebellion against the existing law is the saddling of the right to a child with the obligation to become the servant of a man.

George Bernard Shaw

Do not breed. Nothing gives less pleasure than childbearing. Pregnancies are damaging to health, spoil the figure, wither the charms, and it's the cloud of uncertainty for ever hanging over these events that darkens a husband's mood.

Marquis de Sade

We've begun to long for the pitter patter of little feet. So we bought a dog. Well, it's cheaper and you get more feet.

Rita Rudner

I get those maternal feelings. Like when I'm lying on the couch and can't reach the remote. 'Boy, a kid would be nice, right now.'

Kathleen Madigan

Baby Making

My ultimate fantasy is to entice a man to my bedroom, put a gun
to his head and say, 'Make babies or die.'

Ruby Wax

I like trying to get pregnant. I'm not so sure about childbirth.

George Eliot

As soon as my husband and I can be in the same city, at the same
time, I'd say we have a better chance of actually having children.

Sarah Jessica Parker

When all is said and done, monotony may after all be the best
condition for creation.

Margaret Sackville

It is said that life begins when the foetus can exist apart from
its mother. By this definition, many people in Hollywood are
legally dead.

Jay Leno

A Bumpy Ride Pregnancy

If pregnancy were a book they would cut the last two chapters.

Nora Ephron

Women are nothing but machines for producing children.

Napoleon Bonaparte

I positively think that ladies who are always enceinte quite disgusting; it is more like a rabbit or a guinea pig than anything else and really it is not very nice.

Queen Victoria

Being slightly paranoid is like being slightly pregnant – it tends to get worse.

Molly Irvins

Being pregnant is an occupational hazard of being a wife.

Queen Victoria

Advice to expectant mothers: you must remember that when you are pregnant, you are eating for two. But you must also remember that the other one of you is about the size of a golf ball, so let's not go overboard with it. I mean a lot of pregnant women eat as though the other person they're eating for is Orson Welles.

Dave Barry

Labour Intensive

Delivery is the wrong word to describe the childbearing process.
Delivery is, 'Here's your pizza.' Takes thirty minutes or less.
Exorcism, I think, is more apt: 'Please! Get the hell out of my body!'
Jeff Stilson

Childbirth is no more a miracle than eating food and a turd
coming out of your ass.
Bill Hicks

I'm not interested in being wonder woman in the delivery room.
Give me drugs.
Madonna

My mother groaned, my father wept, into the dangerous world
I leapt; helpless, naked, piping loud, like a fiend hid in cloud.
William Blake

A male gynaecologist is like an auto mechanic who never owned
a car.
Carrie Snow

Childbearing is glorified in part because women die from it.
Andrea Dworkin

These wretched babies don't come until they are ready.
Queen Elizabeth II

Good work Mary, we all knew you had it in you.
Dorothy Parker

He doesn't speak, the newborn? Why his entire being shouts out, 'Don't touch me! Don't touch me!' And yet at the same time, imploringly, begging, 'Don't leave me! Don't leave me!'… This is birth. This is the torture, the Calvary.
Dr Frederick Leboyer, French obstetrician

A woman when she is in travail hath sorrow, because her hour is come: but as soon as she is delivered of the child, she remembereth no more the anguish, for joy that a man is born into the world.
John 16:21

If men had to have babies they would only ever have one each.
Princess Diana

Although present on the occasion, I have no clear recollection of the events leading up to it.
Winston Churchill, discussing his own birth

I was born at the age of 12 on the Metro-Goldwyn-Mayer lot.
Judy Garland

As they started to clean it off … I went over to my wife, kissed her gently on the lips, and said, 'Darling, I love you very much. You just had a lizard.'

Bill Cosby

My wife – God bless her – was in labour for thirty-two hours. And I was faithful to her the entire time.

Jonathan Katz

Open All Hours

BREASTFEEDING

There are three reasons for breastfeeding: the milk is always at the right temperature; it comes in attractive containers; and the cat can't get it.

Irene Chalmers

There is no finer investment for any community than putting milk into babies.

Winston Churchill

My opinion is that anyone offended by breastfeeding is staring too hard.

Dave Allen

No one who has seen a baby sinking back satiated from the breast and falling asleep with flushed cheeks and a blissful smile can escape the reflection that this picture persists as a prototype of the expression of sexual satisfaction in later life.

Sigmund Freud

The babe at first feeds upon the mother's bosom, but is always on her heart.

Henry Ward Beecher

You cannot have power for good without having power for evil too. Even mother's milk nourishes murderers as well as heroes.

George Bernard Shaw

Anyone who has breastfed knows two things for sure: the baby wants to be fed at the most inopportune times, and in the most inopportune places, and the baby will prevail.

Anna Quindlen

There is no dream of love, however ideal it may be, which does not end up with a fat, greedy baby hanging from the breast.

Charles Baudelaire

In at the Deep End

BRINGING HOME BABY

I remember leaving the hospital thinking, 'Wait, are they just going to let me walk off with him? I don't know beans about babies. I don't have a licence to do this.'

Anne Tyler

The worst feature of a new baby is its mother singing.

Kin Hubbard

The hot, moist smell of babies fresh from naps.

Barbara Lazear Ascher

I understood once I held a baby in my arms, why some people have the need to keep having them.

Spalding Gray

It is true that you may occasionally overhear a mother say, 'Children must have their naps, it is mother who knows best.' When what she really means is that she needs a rest.

Anon.

Holding your firstborn, your wife looks at you through different eyes, a traveller from another country. The mothering cues are clearly rooted very deep in the female psyche.

Charlton Heston

My mother says I didn't open my eyes for eight days after I was born, but when I did, the first thing I saw was an engagement ring. I was hooked.

Elizabeth Taylor

When you have a baby, you set off an explosion in your marriage, and when the dust settles, your marriage is different from what it was. Not better, necessarily; but different.

Nora Ephron

What is the use of a newborn child?

Benjamin Franklin

Athens holds sway over all Greece; I dominate Athens; my wife dominates me; our newborn son dominates her.

Themistocles, explaining why his newborn son ruled all Greece

Someone once told me that children are like heroin. You always want more. Yet firstborns are special because you'll never have your first child again.

Sarah Jessica Parker

The conscientious mother of this age approaches the birth of her first baby with two ideas firmly in mind. One is that she will raise the baby by schedule. The other, that she will not let it suck its thumb.

Gladys D. Schultz

If you desire to drain to the dregs the fullest cup of scorn and hatred that a fellow human being can pour out for you, let a young mother hear you call dear baby 'it'.

Jerome K. Jerome

I could still remember how having a two-day-old baby makes you feel faintly sorry for everyone else, stuck in their wan unmiraculous lives.

Marni Jackson

A soiled baby, with a neglected nose, cannot be conscientiously regarded as a thing of beauty.

Mark Twain, replying to a young mother

A baby is a blank cheque made payable to the human race.

Barbara Christine Seifert

We learn from experience. You never wake up a second baby just to see it smile.

Anon.

What good mothers ... instinctively feel like doing for their babies is usually best after all.

Benjamin Spock

The naïve notion that a mother naturally acquires the complex skills of childrearing simply because she has given birth now seems as absurd to me as enrolling in a nine-month class in composition and imagining that at the end of the course you are now prepared to begin writing War and Peace.

Mary Kay Blakely

Post-natal Degeneration

It's a huge change for your body. You don't even want to look in the mirror after you've had a baby, because your stomach is just hanging there like a Shar-Pei.

Cindy Crawford

The breasts go first, and then the waist and then the butt. Nobody ever tells you that you get a butt when you get pregnant.

Elle Macpherson

CHARLOTTE: What kind of diet book are you looking for?
MIRANDA: I don't know. Something with a title like 'How to Lose That Baby Fat by Sitting on Your Ass'.

Sex and the City

People said I'd slim down quickly. Nobody told me it was because I'd never have time to eat.

Anon.

You've been a fantastic mother. You've let them ruin your figure. Your stomach is stretched beyond recognition, you've got tits down to your knees and what for, for God's sake?

***Patsy to Edina*, Absolutely Fabulous**

Wishful Thinking

SEX AFTER CHILDBIRTH

It's so long since I've had sex, I've forgotten who ties up who.

Joan Rivers

No woman needs intercourse; few women escape it.

Andrea Dworkin

Vibrators. I think they are great. They keep you out of stupid sex.
I'd pitch them to anyone.

Anne Heche

Older women are best, because they always think they may be
doing it for the last time.

Ian Fleming

Before we make love my husband takes a painkiller.

Joan Rivers

My best birth control now is just to leave the lights on.

Joan Rivers

The best contraception for old people is nudity.

Phyllis Diller

Contraceptives should be used on every conceivable occasion.

Spike Milligan

Have you noticed that all the people in favour of birth control are already born?

Benny Hill

It is now quite lawful for a Catholic woman to avoid pregnancy by a resort to mathematics, though she is still forbidden to resort to physics and chemistry.

Henry Louis Mencken

When my mom found my diaphragm, I told her it was a bathing cap for my cat.

Liz Winston

Given a choice between hearing my daughter say 'I'm pregnant' or 'I used a condom', most mothers would get up in the middle of the night and buy them themselves.

Joycelyn Elders

The best form of contraception is a pill – held firmly between the knees.

Anon.

I'm glad I'm a woman because I don't have to worry about getting men pregnant.

Nell Dunn

Driving You Potty

Laughter is like changing a baby's diaper. It doesn't permanently solve any problems, but it makes things more acceptable for a while.

Anon.

One year, I'd completely lost my bearings trying to follow potty training instruction from a psychiatric expert. I was stuck on step one, which stated without an atom of irony: 'Before you begin, remove all stubbornness from the child.'

Mary Kay Blakely

Like many other women, I could not understand why every man who changed a diaper has felt compelled to write a book about it.

Barbara Ehrenreich

Most men cannot change a diaper without subsequently renting an airplane that trails a banner that says 'I CHANGED A DIAPER.'

Anna Quindlen

Diaper backward spells repaid. Think about it.

Marshall Mcluhan

A bit of talcum
Is always walcum.

Ogden Nash

Kids: Who'd Have 'Em?

There is no reciprocity. Men love women, women love children.
Children love hamsters.

Alice Thomas Ellis

Children ask better questions than adults. 'May I have a cookie?'
'Why is the sky blue?' and 'What does a cow say?' are far more
likely to elicit a cheerful response than 'Where is your manuscript?'
'Why haven't you called?' and 'Who's your lawyer?'

Fran Lebowitz

Being a child is horrible. It is slightly better than being a tree
or a piece of heavy machinery but not half as good as being
a domestic cat.

Julie Burchill

Toddlers are more likely to eat healthy food if they find it
on the floor.

Jan Blaustone

Perhaps parents would enjoy their children more if they stopped
to realize that the film of childhood can never be run through for
a second showing.

Evelyn Nown

Whether your child is 3 or 13, don't rush in to rescue him until you know he's done all he can to rescue himself.

Barbara F. Meltz

No animal is so inexhaustible as an excited infant.

Amy Leslie

Anyone who thinks the art of conversation is dead ought to tell a child to go to bed.

Anon.

I love this child. Red-haired – patient and gentle like her mother – fey and funny like her father. When she giggles I can hear him when he and I were young. I am part of this child. It may be only because we share genes and that therefore smell familiar to each other … But for now, it's jelly beans and 'Old MacDonald' that unite us.

Robert Fulghum

Even when freshly washed and relieved of all obvious confections, children tend to be sticky.

Fran Lebowitz

Maternal Moments

There is only one pretty child in the world, and every mother has it.

Chinese proverb

We've begun to raise daughters more like sons ... but few have the courage to raise our sons more like our daughters.

Gloria Steinem

What did that mean, to kiss? You put your face up like that to say goodnight and then his mother put her face down. That was to kiss. His mother put her lips on his cheek; her lips were soft and they wetted his cheek; and they made a tiny little noise: kiss. Why did people do that with their two faces?

James Joyce

Parents of young children should realize that few people, and maybe no one, will find their children as enchanting as they do.

Barbara Walters

To nourish children and raise them against odds is in any time, any place, more valuable than to fix bolts in cars or design nuclear weapons.

Marilyn French

The rules for parents are three ... love, limit, and let them be.

Elaine M. Ward

Whoever Said …

… it takes about six weeks to get back to normal after you've had a baby … doesn't know that once you're a mother, normal is history.

… if you're a good mother, your child will turn out good … must think a child comes with directions and a guarantee.

… 'Good mothers never raise their voices'… never came out the back door just in time to see her child hit a golf ball through the neighbour's window.

… you don't need an education to be a mother … has never helped a fourth grader with his maths homework.

… you can't love a fifth child as much as you love the first … doesn't have five children.

… a mother can stop worrying after her child gets married … doesn't know that marriage adds a new son or daughter-in-law to a mother's heartstrings.

… your mother knows you love her, so you don't need to tell her … isn't a mother.

The Wonder Years

When I was a girl I only had two friends, and they were imaginary. And they would only play with each other.

Rita Rudner

My mother's obsession with the good scissors always scared me a bit. It implied that somewhere in the house there lurked: the evil scissors.

Tony Martin

When you've seen a nude infant doing a backward somersault you know why clothing exists.

Stephen Fry

A sweater is a garment worn by a child when the mother feels chilly.

Barbara Johnson

Boys are found everywhere – on top of, underneath, inside of, climbing on, swinging from, running around or jumping to. Mothers love them, little girls hate them, older sisters and brothers tolerate them, adults ignore them and Heaven protects them.

Alan Marshall Beck

Things You Should Never Say to a Mother

I wouldn't let my child speak to me like that.

Is one of your twins smarter than the other?

Why don't you dress your twins the same?

Is your baby supposed to be that fat?

She doesn't look like you – is she adopted?

Are you pregnant again?

Do you know who the real mum is?

You've got your hands full.

Skool Rools

Parents learn a lot from their children about coping with life.

Muriel Spark

The mother's heart is the child's schoolroom.

Henry Ward Beecher

Children learn to smile from their parents.

Shinichi Suzuki

You may have tangible wealth untold; caskets of jewels and coffers of gold. Richer than I you can never be, I had a mother who read to me.

Strickland Gillian

I never went to school beyond the third grade, but my mother taught me the difference between right and wrong.

Joe Lewis

I hated school. Even to this day, when I see a school bus it's just depressing to me. The poor little kids.

Dolly Parton

Mums are not so much concerned about education, paediatrics, child poverty, law and order and the arms race as about Emily and Robert and Imram and Njoroge. Which is, after all, the same thing.

Clare D'Arcy

It's a mistake to think that once you're done with school you need never learn anything new.

Sophia Loren

The kids were very young and I didn't want to be one of those mums who turn up at the schoolyard covered in tattoos.

Sharon Osbourne

My mother … believed fiction gave one an unrealistic view of the world. Once she caught me reading a novel and chastised me: 'Never let me catch you doing that again, remember what happened to Emma Bovary.'

Angela Carter

'Don't teach my boy poetry,' an English mother recently wrote the Provost of Harrow. 'Don't teach my boy poetry; he is going to stand for Parliament.' Well, perhaps she was right – but if more politicians knew poetry, and more poets knew politics, I am convinced the world would be a little better place to live.

Senator John F. Kennedy

I suppose it is because nearly all children go to school nowadays, and have things arranged for them, that they seem so forlornly unable to produce their own ideas.

Agatha Christie

Everyone is in awe of the lion tamer in a cage with half a dozen lions – everyone but a school bus driver.

Anon.

Rarely is the question asked: is our children learning?

George W. Bush

I was coming home from kindergarten – well mom told me it was kindergarten. I found out later I had been working in a factory for ten years. It's good for a kid to know how to make gloves.

Ellen DeGeneres

Mothers' Classics and Clichés

Someday your face will freeze like that!

What if everyone jumped off a cliff … Would you do it, too?

You're going to put your eye out with that thing!

Don't put that in your mouth … you don't know where it's been.

If I have to get out of this chair!

Don't eat that, you'll get worms!

A little soap and water never killed anyone!

You could have been dead in a ditch for all I knew!

You'd lose your head if it wasn't attached to your shoulders!

The Other Mother

Only Adam had no mother-in-law. That's how we know he lived in paradise.

Old Yiddish saying

I told my mother-in-law that my house was her house, and she said, 'Get the hell off my property.'

Joan Rivers

Having a baby changes the way you view your in-laws. I love it when they come to visit now. They can hold the baby and I can go out.

Matthew Broderick

What a marvellous place to drop one's mother-in-law!

Marshal Foch, remarking on the Grand Canyon

But there, everything has its drawbacks, as the man said when his mother-in-law died, and they came down upon him for the funeral expenses.

Jerome K. Jerome

To have one's mother-in-law in the country when one lives in Paris, and vice versa, is one of those strokes of luck that one encounters only too rarely.

Honoré de Balzac

Honolulu, it's got everything. Sand for the children, sun for the wife, sharks for the wife's mother.

Ken Dodd

Like the man who threw a stone at a bitch, but hit his step-mother, on which he exclaimed, 'Not so bad!'

Plutarch

Mummy, Where Did I Come From?

I didn't know how babies were made until I was pregnant with my fourth child.

Loretta Lynn

I blame my mother for my poor sex life. All she told me was 'the man goes on top and the woman underneath'. For three years my husband and I slept in bunk beds.

Joan Rivers

If sex is such a natural phenomenon, how come there are so many books on how to do it?

Bette Midler

'Do you know who made you?' 'Nobody as I knows on,' said the child, with a short laugh. The idea appeared to amuse her considerably; for her eyes twinkled, and she added, 'I 'spect I growed. Don't think nobody never made me.'

Harriet Beecher Stowe

Hormone Hell

As a teenager you are at the last stage in your life when you will
be happy to hear that the phone is for you.

Fran Lebowitz

Children aren't happy with nothing to ignore, And that's what
parents were created for.

Ogden Nash

Teenage boys, goaded by their surging hormones, run in packs
like the primal horde. They have only a brief season of
exhilarating liberty between control by their mothers and
control by their wives.

Camille Paglia

It is better to be black than gay, because when you're black you
don't have to tell your mother.

Charles Pierce

At 14 you don't need sickness or death for tragedy.

Jessamyn West

Never lend your car to anyone to whom you have given birth.

Erma Bombeck

Raising teenagers is like nailing Jell-o to a tree.

Anon.

Mothers of teenagers know why animals eat their young.

Anon.

An unsupervised teenager with a modem is as dangerous as an unsupervised teenager with a gun.

Gail Thackeray

At the moment that a boy of 13 is turning toward girls, a girl of 13 is turning on her mother. This girl can get rather unreasonable, often saying such comical things as 'Listen, this is my life!'

Bill Cosby

Adolescence is a period of rapid changes. Between the ages of 12 and 17, for example, it can age a mother by as much as twenty years.

Anon.

One mother … was taken aback when she called, as her daughter was going out the door, 'Have a good time,' and her daughter angrily replied, 'Stop telling me what to do!'

Nancy Samalin

Warnings about the 'wrong crowd'… means different things in different places. In Fort Wayne, for example, the wrong crowd meant hanging out with liberal Democrats. In Connecticut, it meant kids who weren't planning to get a PhD from Yale.

Mary Kay Blakely

From the teenager's perspective, remarriage can feel like a hostile takeover.

Laurence Steinberg and Ann Levine

Are you there God? It's me, Margaret. I just told my mother I want a bra. Please help me grow God. You know where. I want to be like everyone else.

Judy Blume

Heredity is what makes parents look at their teenage children and question each other.

Barbara Adams

Alligators have the right idea. They eat their young.

Eve Arden

Mummy's Boy

Few misfortunes can befall a boy which bring worse consequences than to have a really affectionate mother.

Somerset Maugham

The only time a woman really succeeds in changing a man is when he is a baby.

Natalie Wood

Let France have good mothers, and she will have good sons.

Napoleon Bonaparte

The God to whom little boys say their prayers has a face very like their mothers.

James Matthew Barrie

Mother is far too clever to understand anything she does not like.

Arnold Bennett

A boy's best friend is his mother.

Joseph Stefano, Psycho

The one thing a lawyer won't question is the legitimacy of his mother.

W.C. Fields

Even a secret agent can't lie to a Jewish mother.

Peter Malkin

Oh, Mother, you go home too early!
**Edward Albee, in response to his mother's disbelief of the conversations
between the characters in Who's Afraid of Virginia Woolf?**

Never throw stones at your mother,
You'll be sorry for it when she's dead,
Never throw stones at your mother,
Throw bricks at your father instead.

Brendan Behan

It takes a woman twenty years to make a man of her son,
and another woman twenty minutes to make a fool of him.

Helen Rowland

My mother had to send me to the movies with my birth
certificate, so that I wouldn't have to pay the extra fifty
cents that the adults had to pay.

Kareem Abdul-Jabar, NBA basketball player

If your mother tells you to do a thing, it is wrong to reply that
you won't. It is better and more becoming to intimate that you
will do as she bids you, and then afterwards act quietly in the
matter according to the dictates of your better judgement.

Mark Twain

There was never a great man who had not a great mother.

Olive Schreiner

If that's the world's smartest man, God help us.

Lucille Feynman, talking about her son, a Nobel laureate labelled the world's smartest man by Omni magazine

Two of the most difficult tasks a writer can undertake, to write the truth about himself and about his mother.

Time magazine, on Frank O'Connor's An Only Child

If Madonna's child is a boy, it'll be the longest relationship she's ever had with a man.

Craig Kilborn

My birth neither shook the German Empire nor caused much of an upheaval in the home. It pleased mother ...

Conrad Veidt

I blame Rousseau, myself. 'Man is born free' indeed. Man is not born free, he is born attached to his mother by a cord and is not capable of looking after himself for at least seven years (seventy in some cases).

Katharine Whitehorn

PHILIP DRUMMOND: Mother gets very impatient if she's kept waiting: I was born three days late; she didn't speak to me for a year.

Diff 'rent Strokes

When I was born, my mother mistook the afterbirth as my twin; and the cuter one, too.

Manny Coon, **The Kids in the Hall**

Men are what their mothers made them.

Ralph Waldo Emerson

I don't care how much of a lama he is, he still needs his mother.

Maria Torres, Spanish woman whose 10-year-old son is believed by Tibetan monks to be a reincarnated lama.

Famous Sons

I wiggle my shoulders, I shake my legs, I walk up and down the stage, I hop around on one foot. But I never bump and grind. I'd never do anything vulgar before an audience. My mother would never allow it.

Elvis Presley

I was the fattest baby in Clark County, Arkansas. They put me in the newspaper. It was like a prize turnip.

Billy Bob Thornton

When I was a child, my mother said to me, 'If you become a soldier, you'll be a general. If you become a monk you'll end up as the pope.' Instead I became a painter and wound up as Picasso.

Pablo Picasso

My mother loved children – she would have given anything if I had been one.

Groucho Marx

It seems to me that my mother was the most splendid woman I ever knew … I have met a lot of people knocking around the world since, but I have never met a more thoroughly refined woman than my mother. If I have amounted to anything, it will be due to her.

Charles Chaplin

My mother has always been unhappy with what I do. She would rather I do something nicer, like be a bricklayer.

Mick Jagger

It's our money, and we're free to spend it any way we please.

Rose Kennedy, on her son John F. Kennedy's presidential campaign

I've never struck a woman in my life, not even my own mother.

W.C. Fields

He wrote me sad Mother's Day stories. He'd always kill me in the stories and tell me how bad he felt about it. It was enough to bring a tear to a mother's eye.

Connie Zastoupil, mother of Quentin Tarantino

The whole motivation for any performer is, 'Look at me, Ma!'

Lenny Bruce

Looking back on my own childhood, after the infant years were over, I do not believe that I ever felt love for any mature person, except my mother …

George Orwell

Hey, Ma, your bad boy did good!

Rocky Graziano, **Rocky**

Me and My Girl

Every bride has to learn it's not her wedding but her mother's.

Saint Augustine

As long as a woman can look ten years younger than her own daughter, she is perfectly satisfied.

Oscar Wilde

If my daughter Liza wants to become an actress, I'll do everything to help her.

Judy Garland

A fluent tongue is the only thing a mother don't like her daughter to resemble her in.

Richard Brinsley-Sheridan

To me, luxury is to be at home with my daughter, and the occasional massage doesn't hurt.

Olivia Newton-John

A busy mother makes slothful daughters.

Portuguese proverb

There is a point when you aren't as much mom and daughter as you are adults and friends. It doesn't happen for everyone – but it did for mom and me.

Jamie Lee Curtis

It is not that I half knew my mother. I knew half of her: the lower half – her lap, legs, feet, her hands and wrists as she bent forward.

Flann O'Brien

Unlike the mother–son relationship, a daughter's relationship with her mother is something akin to bungee diving ... there is an invisible emotional cord that snaps her back.

Victoria Secunda

Doesn't that show what an old man I am, when I can say to a mother 'I love your daughter,' and not get the reply 'What are your intentions, and what is your income?'

Lewis Carroll

My daughter is every mother's child and every mother is the mother of my child.

Glen Close

The Depression era generation of mothers … believed …
the worst fate was to be independent. Their daughters, jolted
by Vietnam, the sexual revolution, and feminism, were largely
committed to themselves. For them, the worst fate was to be
dependent.

Victoria Secunda

[My daughter] says she wants to marry a rich man, so she can
have a Porsche. My rejoinder always is: 'Go out and get rich
yourself, so you can buy your own.'

Carol Royce

Oh my son's my son till he gets him a wife,
But my daughter's my daughter all her life.

Dinah Maria Mulock Craik

The only other person I've apologized to is my mother
and that was court ordered.

Karen, **Will and Grace**

Mother, just because I wear trackies and play sports does
not make me a lesbian!

Jules, **Bend It Like Beckham**

Having It All

WORKING MUMS

Touring full-time with children is a study in sleep deprivation: the day never ends! Many times on the road we do a sound check, then everybody goes to dinner. If I'm eating with the kids, I go back to my dressing room and fall into a dead sleep until it's time for me to get up and put my stage clothes on.

Amy Grant

Any sane person would have left long ago. But I cannot. I have my sons.

Princess Diana

At work you think of the children you have left at home. At home you think of the work you've left unfinished. Such a struggle is unleashed within yourself. Your heart is rent.

Golda Meir

The phrase 'working mother' is redundant.

Jane Sellman

I have a brain and a uterus, and I use both.

Patricia Schroeder, US Congresswoman, on being an elected official and a mother

I was standing in the schoolyard waiting for a child when another mother came up to me. 'Have you found work yet?' she asked. 'Or are you still just writing?'

Anne Tyler

Clearly, society has a tremendous stake in insisting on a woman's natural fitness for the career of mother: the alternatives are all too expensive.

Ann Oakley

I have often felt that I cheated my children a little. I was never so totally theirs as most mothers are. I gave to audiences what belonged to my children, got back from audiences the love my children longed to give me.

Eleanor Roosevelt

I'm tired of earning my own living, paying my own bills, raising my own child … Self-sufficiency is exhausting. Autonomy is lonely. It's so hard to be a feminist if you are a woman.

Jane O'Reilly

It's hard being a working mum, but we have fun. We do shows together. We play all the parts in The Wizard of Oz. She watches the show, and does imitations of Julie Kavner.

Tracey Ullman

Aspirational Mums

Mothers all want their sons to grow up to be president, but they don't want them to become politicians in the process.

John F. Kennedy

All mothers think their children are oaks, but the world never lacks for cabbages.

Robertson Davies

I want my children to have all the things I couldn't afford. Then I want to move in with them.

Phyllis Diller

Mama exhorted her children at every opportunity to 'Jump at de sun'. We might not land on the sun, but at least we would get off the ground.

Zora Neale Hurston

If I have children I am going to make sure people don't ask them, 'Are you going to be an actor?' My mother said I could be anything I wanted except a policeman.

Kate Beckinsale

Thank you to Martin Scorsese – I hope my son will marry
your daughter.

Cate Blanchett

My mother was against me being an actress until I introduced her
to Frank Sinatra.

Angie Dickinson

Every beetle is a gazelle in the eyes of its mother.

Arab proverb

My mother married a very good man … and she is not at all
keen on my doing the same.

George Bernard Shaw

Dare to Be Different

UNCONVENTIONAL FAMILIES

You hear a lot of dialogue on the death of the American family.
Families aren't dying. They're merging into big conglomerates.

Erma Bombeck

What is free time? I'm a single mother. My free moments are
filled with loving my little girl.

Roma Downey

Yes, single-parent families are different from two-parent families.
And urban families are different from rural ones, and families
with six kids and a dog are different from one-child, no-pet
households. But even if there is only one adult presiding at the
dinner table, yours is every bit as much a real family as
the Waltons.

Marge Kennedy

People talk about dysfunctional families; I've never seen any
other kind.

Sue Grafton

I worry about people who get born nowadays, because they get born into such tiny families – sometimes into no family at all. When you're the only pea in the pod, your parents are likely to get you confused with the Hope Diamond.

Russell Baker

Adopted kids are such a pain. You have to teach them how to look like you.

Gilda Radnor

I married Nicholas Ray, the director. People yawned. Later on I married his son, and from the press's reaction – you'd have thought I was committing incest or robbing the cradle!

Gloria Grahame

The Birds Have Flown

It kills you to see them grow up. But I guess it would kill
you quicker if they didn't.

Barbara Kingsolver

The best way to keep children at home is to make the home
atmosphere pleasant, and let the air out of the tyres.

Dorothy Parker

Until I got married, when I used to go out, my mother said
goodbye to me as though I was emigrating.

Thora Hird

Mothers need transfusions fairly often – phone calls, letters,
bright postcards from the Outer Hebrides.

Heulwen Roberts

A mother never realizes that her children are no longer children.

Holbrook Jackson

Hello, Arthur. This is your mother. Do you remember me? …
Someday you'll get married and have children of your own and,
honey, when you do, I only pray that they'll make you suffer the
way you're making me. That's a mother's prayer.'

Mike Nichols

I became the butterfly. I got out of the cocoon, and I flew.
Lynn Redgrave, describing leaving home and moving to California

Kids are cute, babies are cute, puppies are cute. The little things
are cute. See, nature did this on purpose so that we would want
to take care of our young. Made them cute, tricked us. Then
gradually they get older and older, until one day your mother sits
you down and says, 'You know, I think you're ugly enough to get
your own apartment.'

Cathy Ladman

Anyone for Botox?

MUMS ON AGEING

Women over 50 don't have babies because they would put them down and forget where they left them.

Anon.

The woman who tells her age is either too young to have anything to lose or too old to have anything to gain.

Chinese proverb

The really frightening thing about middle age is knowing you'll grow out of it.

Doris Day

Only in America do these peasants, our mothers, get their hair dyed platinum at the age of 60, and walk up and down Collins Avenue in Florida in pedal pushers and mink stoles – and with opinions on every subject under the sun. It isn't their fault they were given a gift like speech – look, if cows could talk, they would say things just as idiotic.

Philip Roth

I refuse to admit that I am more than 52, even if that does make my sons illegitimate.

Nancy Astor

Maybe it's true that life begins at 50 … but everything else starts to wear out, fall out or spread out.

Phyllis Diller

You're never too old to grow up.

Shirley Conran

Mothers are inclined to feel limp at 50. This is because the children have taken most of her stuffing to build their nests.

Samantha Armstrong

Old age ain't no place for sissies.

Bette Davis

I refuse to think of them as chin hairs. I think of them as stray eyebrows.

Janette Barber

Old age is like a plane flying through a storm. Once you're aboard, there's nothing you can do.

Golda Meir

When you made a face and your mother said, 'Be careful your face might freeze that way,' she was right. It just takes longer than you think.

Johanna Newell

I have flabby thighs, but fortunately my stomach covers them.

Joan Rivers

I don't plan to grow old gracefully. I plan to have face lifts until my ears meet.

Rita Rudner

At 50 you have the choice of keeping your face or your figure, and it's much better to keep your face.

Barbara Cartland

Grandmas

If your baby is beautiful and perfect, never cries or fusses, sleeps on schedule and burps on demand, an angel all the time, you're the grandma.

Theresa Bloomingdale

Why do grandparents and grandchildren get along so well? They have the same enemy – the mother.

Claudette Colbert

My grandmother was a very tough woman. She buried three husbands and two of them were just napping.

Rita Rudner

We have become a grandmother.

Margaret Thatcher

The simplest toy, one which even the youngest child can operate, is called a grandparent.

Sam Levenson

Being pretty on the inside means you don't hit your brother and you eat up all your peas – that's what my grandma taught me.

Lord Chesterfield

Grandchildren don't make a man feel old; it's the knowledge he's married to a grandmother.

G. Norman Collie

A grandmother is a babysitter who watches the kids instead of television.

Anon.

Grandmas are people who take delight in hearing babies breathing into the telephone.

Anon.

When the grandmothers of today hear the word 'Chippendales', they don't necessarily think of chairs.

Jean Kerr

You have to stay in shape. My grandmother, she started walking five miles a day when she was 60. She's 97 today and we don't know where the hell she is.

Ellen DeGeneres

One of life's greatest mysteries is how the boy who wasn't good enough to marry your daughter can be the father of the smartest grandchild in the world

Jewish proverb

Maybe there is no actual place called hell. Maybe hell is just having to listen to our grandmothers breathe through their noses when they're eating sandwiches.

Jim Carrie

War and Peas

MUMS, MENUS AND MEALTIMES

I do not like broccoli and I haven't liked it since I was a little
kid and my mother made me eat it. Now I am President of the
United States and I am not going to eat any more broccoli.

George Bush

My mother's menu consisted of two choices: take it or leave it.

Buddy Hackett

In general my children refuse to eat anything that hasn't danced
on television.

Erma Bombeck

My mother was a good recreational cook, but what she basically
believed about cooking was that if you worked hard and
prospered, someone else would do it for you.

Nora Ephron

The most remarkable thing about my mother is that for thirty
years she served the family nothing but leftovers. The original
meal has never been found.

Calvin Trillin

I don't even butter my bread; I consider that cooking.

Katherine Cebrian

Chicken soup: an ancient miracle drug containing equal parts of erythromycin, cocaine, interferon and TLC. The only ailment chicken soup can't cure is neurotic dependence on one's mother.

Arthur Naiman

As a mother I am often confused ... One day I tell them to eat what they like, their bodies know intuitively what they need; and the next I say, 'OK, that's it – no more junk food in this house!'

Martha Boesing

I refuse to believe that trading recipes is silly. Tuna fish casserole is at least as real as corporate stock.

Barbara Harrison

Even while I protest the assembly-line production of our food, our songs, our language, and eventually our souls, I know that it was a rare home that baked good bread in the old days. Mother's cooking was with rare exceptions poor.

John Steinbeck

Life is too short to stuff a mushroom.

Shirley Conran

For a long time I thought coq au vin meant love in a lorry.

Victoria Wood

Carrots do something for children's vision. Kids can spot carrots no matter how you disguise them.

Anon.

Mother's Little Helper

MUMS ON PROZAC

A friend of mine confused her Valium with her birth control pills.
She has fourteen kids but she doesn't really care.

Anon.

The worker can unionize, go out on strike; mothers are
divided from each other in homes, tied to their children by
compassionate bonds; our wildcat strikes have most often taken
the form of physical or mental breakdown.

Adrienne Rich

Mothers are all slightly insane.

J.D. Salinger

Children are the anchors that hold a mother to life.

Sophocles

Don't be afraid of me because I'm coming back from the
mental hospital – I'm your mother.

Allen Ginsberg

I used to be excellent. Since having a baby I couldn't tell you what day it is.

Gwyneth Paltrow

I tried to commit suicide by sticking my head in the oven, but there was a cake in it.

Lesley Boone

If Mr Vincent Price were to be co-starred with Miss Bette Davis in a story by Mr Edgar Allan Poe directed by Mr Roger Corman, it could not fully express the pent-up violence and depravity of a single day in the life of the average family.

Quentin Crisp

This is Dr Niles Crane, filling in for my ailing brother, Dr Frasier Crane. Although I feel perfectly qualified to fill Frasier's radio shoes, I should warn you that while Frasier is a Freudian, I am a Jungian. So there'll be no blaming Mother today.

Niles, Frasier

Reality is just a crutch for people who can't cope with drugs.

Lily Tomlin

A Dirty Job, but Someone's Got to Do It!

HOUSEWORK

Cleaning your house while the kids are still growing is like shovelling the walk before it stops snowing.

Phyllis Diller

My mother was an authority on pigsties. 'This is the worst-looking pigsty I have ever seen in my life and I want it cleaned up right now!'

Bill Cosby

How do you know it's time to wash the dishes and clean your house? Look inside your pants. If you find a penis in there, it's not time.

Jo Brand

My second favourite household chore is ironing. My first being hitting my head on the top bunk until I faint.

Erma Bombeck

Any mother could perform the jobs of several air-traffic controllers with ease.

Lisa Alther

You can't get spoiled if you do your own ironing.

Meryl Streep

I am thankful for a lawn that needs mowing, windows that need cleaning and gutters that need fixing because it means I have a home … I am thankful for the piles of laundry and ironing because it means my loved ones are nearby.

Nancie J. Carmody

Nature abhors a vacuum. And so do I.

Anne Gibbons

Don't cook. Don't clean. No man will ever make love to a woman because she waxed the linoleum – 'My God, the floor's immaculate. Lie down you hot bitch.'

Joan Rivers

The Rose Bowl is the only bowl I've ever seen that I didn't have to clean.

Erma Bombeck

Housework can't kill you, but why take a chance?

Phyllis Diller

I hate housework! You make the beds, you do the dishes – and six months later you have to start all over again.

Joan Rivers

Neurotics build castles in the air, psychotics live in them. My mother cleans them.

Rita Rudner

If I'm sitting on the toilet and I'm looking at the grouting on the tiles, that grouting really gets me. Mothers have a thing about grouting.

Sharon Osbourne

My idea of housework is to sweep the room with a glance.

Anon.

Housekeeping is like being caught in a revolving door.

Marcelene Cox

I buried a lot of my ironing in the backyard.

Phyllis Diller

At worst, a house unkempt cannot be so distressing as a life unlived.

Rose Macauley

Have you ever taken anything out of the clothes basket because it had become, relatively, the cleaner thing?

Katharine Whitehorn

Home is the girl's prison and the woman's workhouse.

George Bernard Shaw

Famous Mums

I may be the only mother in America who knows exactly what their child is up to all the time.

Barbara Bush

I live for my sons. I would be lost without them.

Princess Diana

I said I would get better with each baby, and I have.

Demi Moore

When you are a mother, you are never really alone in your thoughts. A mother always has to think twice, once for herself and once for her child.

Sophia Loren

If you bungle raising your children, I don't think whatever else you do well matters very much.

Jacqueline Kennedy Onassis

Since I had the baby I can't tolerate anything violent or sad, I saw The Matrix and I had my eyes closed through a lot of it, though I didn't need to. I would peek, and then think, 'Oh OK, I can see that.'

Lisa Kudrow

I love acting but it's much more fun taking the kids to the zoo.
Nicole Kidman

I've told Billy if I ever caught him cheating, I wouldn't kill him because I love his children and they need a dad. But I would beat him up. I know where all of his sports injuries are.
Angelina Jolie

I'm a mother with two small children, so I don't take as much crap as I used to.
Pamela Anderson

Grown don't mean nothing to a mother. A child is a child. They get bigger, older, but grown. In my heart it don't mean a thing.
Toni Morrison

Mum comes in and says 'I'm working out,' and she'll just be standing there naked doing a dance.
Kelly Osbourne

Be a first-rate version of yourself, not a second-rate version of someone else.
Judy Garland, to her daughter, Liza Minnelli

There is nothing more thrilling in this world, I think, than having a child that is yours, and yet is mysteriously a stranger.
Agatha Christie

I love all my children, but some of them I don't like.
Lillian Carter, mother of President Jimmy Carter

Because I am a mother, I am capable of being shocked: as I never was when I was not one.
Margaret Atwood

Don't call me an icon. I'm just a mother trying to help.
Princess Diana

I am not Superwoman. The reality of my daily life is that I'm juggling a lot of balls in the air ... and sometimes some of the balls get dropped.
Cherie Blair

He's my wonderful, precious, little Buddha. He eats like a champion. He sleeps peacefully and he's the apple of his daddy's eye.
Sharon Stone

The great high of winning Wimbledon lasts for about a week. You go down in the record book, but you don't have anything tangible to hold on to. But having a baby – there isn't any comparison.
Chris Everett Lloyd

I have come, Sire, to complain of one of your subjects who has been so audacious as to kick me in the belly.

Marie Antoinette, telling Louis XVI of France that she was pregnant with their first child

I know I could really kill for my daughter … It's like, that's my lair and nobody messes with my lair.

Whitney Houston

Mick was against it at first but he's OK now. She made $60,000 in one week – what can you say?

Jerry Hall, discussing her daughter's modelling career

I've been through it all baby. I'm Mother Courage.

Elizabeth Taylor

Aurora-Zebedee

NAMING BABY

I'm thinking about naming my first son Emmy so I can say
I've got one. I want Emmy, Oscar and Tony – and my daughter
Grammy.

Noah Wyle

I think my parents were high when they named me.

Jolene Blalock

My mother's very proud of the name she gave me. She thought
it sounded rhythmically better. It doesn't really make a difference
to me what people call me, but since my mother calls me Holly
Marie when she's angry, I prefer just my first name.

Holly Marie Combs

Britney Spears says she plans to name her son London, because
that's where her romance with Kevin Federline began. The couple
were going to name the baby after where it was conceived, but it
was too hard to say Olive Garden Bathroom Floor.

David Spade

My wife wanted to call our daughter Sue, but I felt in my family that was usually a verb.

Dennis Wolfgang

My mother is a botanist, she even named a flower after me. It's called the Bloomin' Idiot.

A.M. radio station

I want to name my kids after people I hate so I can beat them and feel good about it.

Anon.

One thing they never tell you about childraising is that for the rest of your life, at the drop of a hat, you will be expected to know your child's name and how old he or she is.

Erma Bombeck

Famous Daughters

It was no great tragedy being Judy Garland's daughter. I had tremendously interesting childhood years – except they had little to do with being a child.

Liza Minnelli

I wouldn't have turned out the way I was if I didn't have all those old-fashioned values to rebel against.

Madonna

My mother's great. She has the major looks. She could stop you from doing anything, through a closed door even, with a single look. Without saying a word, she has that power to rip out your tonsils.

Whoopi Goldberg

The older I become, the more I think about my mother.

Ingmar Bergman

My mother used to say that there are no strangers, only friends you haven't met yet. She's now in a maximum security twilight home in Australia.

Dame Edna Everage

Mum, have I sung at the Hollywood Bowl?

Charlotte Church

When I was only about 5 or 6 years old, I was standing with my mother in the kitchen at home in Long Beach. I told her flat out that when I grew up I was going to be the best at something. She just smiled and kept peeling potatoes or whatever it was she was doing.

Billie Jean King

If God lets me live, I shall attain more than mummy ever has done, I shall not remain insignificant, I shall work in the world and for mankind!

Anne Frank

I ask people why they have deer heads on their walls. They say, 'Because it's such a beautiful animal.' There you go! I think my mother is attractive, but I have photographs of her.

Ellen DeGeneres

My mother and I could always look out the same window without ever seeing the same thing.

Gloria Swanson

My playground was the theatre. I'd sit and watch my mother pretend for a living. As a young girl, that's pretty seductive

Gwyneth Paltrow

It has always frightened me that people should love her so much.

Queen Mother, of her daughter Elizabeth II as a child

My mother is Irish, my father is black and Venezuelan, and me – I'm tan, I guess.

Mariah Carey

I have a lot of people to thank, and I'm going to be one of those people that tries to mention a lot of names, because I know just two seconds ago my mother and father went completely berserk, and, uh, I'd like to give some other mothers and fathers that opportunity.

Meryl Streep, 55th Academy Awards

Nanny Shenanigans

A babysitter is someone who watches your TV set while your
kids cry themselves to sleep.

Anon.

Our sex life has been ruined since the arrival of our first baby. We
can't be so spontaneous because we don't want the nanny to hear
us. We can't scream and yell like we used to.

Cindy Crawford

There is possibly no guilt in this world to compare with leaving
a sick child with a babysitter. The sitter could be Mother Theresa
and you'd still feel rotten.

Erma Bombeck

She was a beautiful baby. She blew shining bubbles of sound. She
loved motion, loved light, loved colour and music and textures.
When she was just eight months old I had to leave her daytimes
with the woman downstairs to whom she was no miracle at all.

Tillie Olsen

I had a nanny who made me sit in front of a bowl of porridge for three or four days running when I refused to eat it. I remember being very unhappy about that.

Anjelica Huston

I once spent more time writing a note of instructions to a babysitter than I did on my first book.

Erma Bombeck

I should like the whole race of nurses to be abolished. Children should be with their mothers as much as possible in my opinion.

Lewis Carroll

P.I.M.s (Politically Incorrect Mothers)

Mothers' absence notes to their child's teacher:

Please excuse Jimmy for being. It was his father's fault.

Please excuse Jennifer for missing school yesterday. We forgot to get the Sunday paper off the porch, and when we found it Monday, we thought it was Sunday.

My daughter was absent yesterday because she was tired. She spent a weekend with the Marines.

Anon.

I don't think my parents liked me. They put a live teddy bear in my crib.

Woody Allen

My mother had morning sickness after I was born.

Rodney Dangerfield

When I was a little kid we had a sand box. It was a quicksand box. I was an only child ... eventually.

Stephen Wright

The peasants of the Asturias believe that in every litter of wolves there is one pup that is killed by the mother for fear that on growing up it would devour the other little ones.

Victor Hugo

I don't dislike babies, though I think very young ones rather disgusting.

Queen Victoria

And my parents finally realize that I'm kidnapped and they snap into action immediately: They rent out my room.

Woody Allen

My mother never saw the irony in calling me a son-of-a-bitch.

Jack Nicholson

My mother asked me to.

Marc Shreuder, when asked why he had murdered his grandfather

Sometimes when I look at my children, I say to myself, 'Lillian, you should have remained a virgin.'

Lillian Carter (mother of President Jimmy Carter)

It would be better if they told their children, 'Go out and play in traffic.'

Dr Tazewell Banks,
Director of Heart Program, DC General Hospital,
commenting on mothers who feed their children fast food

Parents like the idea of kids, they just don't like their kids.

Morley Saefer

You're *Soooo* Embarrassing ...

Sing out loud in the car even, or especially, if it
embarrasses your children.

Marilyn Penland

One time I ran out of the store and took the bus home by
myself after my mother asked a salesclerk where the
'underpants' counter was. Everyone in the store heard her.
I had no choice.

Phyllis Theroux

To my embarrassment I was born in bed with a woman.

Wilson Mizner

I've had young guys come on to me and I can't do it. I'm
just not into it. I just can't do it ... I wouldn't want to
embarrass or humiliate my kids in any way.

Andie MacDowell

To a teenager there's nothing more embarrassing in the
world than a mother.

Anon.

Mother's Ruin

Gin was mother's milk to her.

George Bernard Shaw

My makeup wasn't smeared, I wasn't dishevelled, I behaved
politely, and I never finished off a bottle, so how could I
be alcoholic?

Betty Ford

'My country, right or wrong', is a thing that no patriot would
think of saying … It is like saying, 'My mother, drunk or sober.'

G. K. Chesterton

I like to have a martini,
Two at the very most –
At three I'm under the table,
At four I'm under the host.

Dorothy Parker

They're trying to put warning labels on liquor saying, 'Caution,
alcohol can be dangerous to pregnant women.' That's ironic. If it
weren't for alcohol, most women wouldn't even be that way.

Anon.

Your Mother Should Know

MOTHERS' ADVICE AND WORDS OF WISDOM

My mother said I must always be intolerant of ignorance but understanding of illiteracy. That some people, unable to go to school, were more educated and more intelligent than college professors.

Maya Angelou

My mother always told me I wouldn't amount to anything because I procrastinate. I said, 'Just wait.'

Judy Tenuta

Hugs can do great amounts of good – especially for children.

Princess Diana

Everybody today seems to be in such a terrible rush, anxious for greater developments and greater riches and so on, so that children have very little time for their parents. Parents have very little time for each other, and in the home begins the disruption of peace of the world.

Mother Theresa

I thought she'd [her mother] offer me some sympathy. Instead she said, 'Don't you ever call me crying again! You wanted to be in this business, so you'd better toughen up.' And I did.

Jennifer Lopez

My momma always said life was like a box of chocolates … you never know what you're gonna get.

Forrest Gump

The doctors told me that I would never walk, but my mother told me I would, so I believed my mother.

Wilma Rudolph, American athlete

My mother said it was simple to keep a man, you must be a maid in the living room, a cook in the kitchen and a whore in the bedroom. I said I'd hire the other two and take care of the bedroom bit.

Jerry Hall

Every man has been brought up with the idea that decent women don't pop in and out of bed; he has always been told by his mother that 'nice girls don't'. He finds, of course, when he gets older that this may be untrue – but only in a certain section of society.

Barbara Cartland

My great-grandfather used to say to his wife, my great-grandmother, who in turn told her daughter, my grandmother, who repeated it to her daughter, my mother, who used to remind her daughter, my own sister, that to talk well and eloquently was a very great art, but that an equally great one was to know the right moment to stop.

Wolfgang Amadeus Mozart

A child's fingers are not scalded by a piece of hot yam which his mother puts into his palm.

African proverb

Be a doctor! Be a lawyer! Be a leper missionary!
Diane Ladd, advising her daughter, Laura Dern, not to act

Mother what is marrying? Spinning, bearing children and crying, daughter.

Spanish proverb

Well it doesn't matter how you feel inside, you know? It's what shows up on the surface that counts. That's what my mother taught me. Take all your bad feelings and push them down, all the way down, past your knees until you're almost walking on them. And then you'll fit in, and you'll be invited to parties, and boys will like you, and happiness will follow.

Marge, **The Simpsons**

Give Me a Break!

HIGH DAYS AND HOLIDAYS

No self-respecting mother would run out of intimidations on the eve of a major holiday.

Erma Bombeck

I stopped believing in Santa Claus when my mother took me to see him in a department store, and he asked for my autograph.

Shirley Temple

By and large, mothers and housewives are the only workers who do not have regular time off. They are the great vacationless class.

Anne Morrow Lindbergh

Christmas … is not an eternal event at all, but a piece of one's home that one carries in one's heart.

Freya Stark

Everyone has the right to go on holiday without the kids if they want to.

Laura Schlessinger

The Back of My Hand

MOTHERS AND DISCIPLINE

Experts say you should never hit your children in anger. When is a good time? When you're feeling festive?

Roseanne Barr

All children have to be deceived if they are to grow up without trauma.

Kazuo Ishiguro

It is not a bad thing that children should occasionally, and politely, put parents in their place.

Colette

Some are kissing mothers and some are scolding mothers, but it is love just the same – and most mothers kiss and scold together.

Pearl S. Buck

Raising children is like chewing on a stone.

Arab proverb

What time I go to bed has zippo to do with what time you go to bed.

Susan Raffy (talking to her son)

Fathers on Mothers

No mother would ever willingly sacrifice her sons for territorial gain, for economic advantage, for ideology.

Ronald Reagan

I sincerely believe that if Bush and Cheney recognized the full humanity of other people's mothers around the world, they wouldn't commit the crimes they commit.

Wallace Shawn

You couldn't fool your mother on the foolingest day of your life if you had an electrified fooling machine.

Homer, **The Simpsons**

I can be a good father but I'm a terrible mother.

Rainier, Prince of Monaco

Sue Ellen, you're a drunk, a tramp, and an unfit mother.

J. R. Ewing, **Dallas**

Mothers on Fathers

When Charles first saw our child Mary, he said all the proper things for a new father. He looked upon the poor little red thing and blurted, 'She's more beautiful than the Brooklyn bridge.'

Helen Hayes

Be a father. Your son has friends his own age; no boy needs a 44-year-old 'pal'.

Ann Landers

If it has tyres or testicles, you're going to have trouble with it.

Linda Furney

My mom said the only reason men are alive is for lawn care and vehicle maintenance.

Tim Allen

No man is responsible for his father. That is entirely his mother's affair.

Margaret Turnball

Mother of God

God could not be everywhere and therefore he made mothers.
Jewish proverb

An ounce of mother is worth a pound of clergy.
Spanish proverb

I regard no man as poor who has a godly mother.
Abraham Lincoln

God will protect us, [my mother] often said to me. 'But to make sure,' she would add, 'carry a heavy club.'
Gypsy Rose Lee

I'm a godmother, that's a great thing to be, a godmother. She calls me god for short, that's cute, I taught her that.
Ellen DeGeneres

I hope my child will be a good Catholic like me.
Madonna

Every mother is like Moses. She does not enter the promised land. She prepares a world she will not see.
Pope Paul VI

Mummy Dearest ...

A man loves his sweetheart the most, his wife the best, but his mother the longest.

Irish proverb

Whenever I'm with my mother, I feel as though I have to spend the whole time avoiding land mines.

Amy Tan

A mother's love for her child is like nothing else in the world. It knows no law, no pity, it dares all things and crushes down remorselessly all that stands in its path.

Agatha Christie

Life began with waking up and loving my mother's face.

George Eliot

Whatever else is unsure in this stinking dunghill of a world a mother's love is not.

James Joyce

My mother lived the latter years of her life in the horrible suspicion that electricity was dripping invisibly all over the house.

James Thurber

Health Issues

The best medicine in the world is a mother's kiss.

Anon.

My father invented a cure for which there was no disease and unfortunately my mother contracted it and died of it.

Victor Borge

You'll have to excuse my mother. She suffered a slight stroke a few years ago which rendered her totally annoying.

Dorothy, **The Golden Girls**

Patient has two teenage children but no other abnormalities.

Written on a patient's medical charts

A woman came to ask the doctor if a woman should have children after 35. I said 35 children is enough for any woman!

Gracie Allen

Kids on Mums

To choose the right mom for your kids you got to find somebody who likes the right stuff. Like if you like sports she should keep the chips and dip coming.

Alan, aged 10

If nobody got married there sure would be a lot of kids to explain, wouldn't there?

Kelvin, aged 8

You gotta tell your mom that she looks pretty even if she looks like a truck.

Ricky, aged 10

If it's your mother, you can kiss her any time. But if it's a new person, you have to ask permission.

Roger, aged 6

God makes mothers out of clouds and angel hair and everything nice in the world – and one dab of mean.

Anon.

From Cradle to Grave

There she was in her bed. Dead. But nobody explained it to me. They told me later that she had gone to America.
Vartan Gregorian, describing his mother's death when he was aged 7

'Jakie, is it my birthday or am I dying?' Her son replied, 'A bit of both, Mum.'
Viscountess Nancy Astor, on her deathbed

Mother died today. Or perhaps it was yesterday, I don't know.
Albert Camus

The mother is everything – she is our consolation in sorrow, our hope in misery, and our strength in weakness. She is the source of love, mercy, sympathy, and forgiveness. He who loses his mother loses a pure soul who blesses and guards him constantly.
Kahlil Gibran

There I sat, in the biting wind, wishing she were gone.
Krapp, speaking of his dying mother, in Samuel Beckett's
Krapp's Last Tape

158

Index

Picture Credits

The publishers would like to thank the following sources for their kind permission to reproduce the pictures in this book:

ALL PHOTOGRAPHS SUPPLIED
BY CORBIS IMAGES

6:	A. Green/Zefa	82:	Gabe Palmer
10:	Rick Gomez	86:	George Shelley
14:	Meeke/Zefa	90:	Poppy Berry/Zefa
18–19:	Rick Gomez	94:	Darius Ramazani/Zefa
22:	Simon Marcus	98:	David Pollack
26:	Dana Tynan	102:	Paul Barton
30:	John Fortunato Photography	106–107:	Randy Faris
34:	Ronnie Kaufman	110:	Ole Graf/Zefa
38:	Elliot/Zefa	114:	John W. Gertz/Zefa
42:	LWA-Dann Tardiff/Zefa	118:	Blasius Erlinger/Zefa
46–47:	A. Green/Zefa	122:	Zave Smith
50–51:	Rick Gomez	126:	Kevin Dodge
54:	John Henley	134:	Kate Mitchell/Zefa
58:	LWA-Sharie Kennedy/Zefa	138:	Steve Prezant
62–63:	Anna Peisl/Zefa	142:	Senthill Kumar
66–67:	Sven Hagolani/Zefa	146:	Tom Stewart
70–71:	Grace/Zefa	150:	Ant Strack
78:	Freitag/Zefa	154–155:	Mango Productions

Every effort has been made to acknowledge correctly and contact the source and/or copyright holder of each picture, and Carlton Books Limited apologises for any unintentional errors or omissions which will be corrected in future editions of this book.